science fair

No Sweat Projects
Shadowy
Science

ALL YOU NEED IS A SHADOW!

PLANET DEXTER®

by Jess Brallier
Illustrated by Bob Staake

Designed by MKR Design/Pat Sweeney.
Cover design by Sammy Yuen and Pat Sweeney.

Published by Planet Dexter, a division of Penguin Putnam Books for Young
Readers, New York.
PLANET DEXTER and the PLANET DEXTER logo are registered trademarks
of Penguin Putnam Inc.
Printed in United States. Published simultaneously in Canada.

Library of Congress Cataloging-in Publication Data.

ISBN 0-448-44089-X   (pb.) A B C D E F G H I J
ISBN 0-448-44097-0   (GB) A B C D E F G H I J

Many of the designations used by manufacturers and sellers to distinguish
their products are claimed as trademarks. Where those designations appear
in this book and Planet Dexter was aware of a trademark claim, the designations have been printed with initial capital letters.

And Now a Message from Our Corporate Lawyer:

"Neither the Publisher nor the Author shall be liable for any
damage that may be caused or sustained as a result of conducting any of the activities in this book without specifically following instructions, conducting the activities without proper super-
vision, or ignoring the cautions contained in the book."

A Shadowy Guide

Introduction

So why does this book exist?

- Need to do a science report or project?

- Looking for a subject that's really interesting *and* fun?

- Searching for an idea that'll impress your teacher *and* amaze your classmates?

- Need a subject that you know really well?

- Hoping to spend very little, or no, money?

- Are you running out of time?

This book is the answer to all those questions.

What this book will not do is your schoolwork. This book gives you ideas and illustrations you can copy, and it even helps get you started on your **research**. But you have to do your own work.

Research is gathering information for your project.

WOW! GATHERING RESEARCH IS FUN!

So? What kind of science project do you need to do?

Reports and Projects Key

Oral Report

Group Activity

Written Report

Exhibit Project

As a student, you may be told to:

or Write a two-page or a five-page report.

or Present a three-minute oral report to the class.

Write a three-page report *and* present a three-minute oral report to the class.

or

Write a three-page report *and* make a poster to be placed in the school cafeteria for parents' evening.

or

Work with three classmates to do a written report *and* present something extra before the whole class.

or

Present an oral report and use stuff like handouts, posters, etc.

Luckily, Shadowy Science Projects! is perfect for any of these. As you use this book, it will tell you how its ideas can be used for different types of reports and projects.

But Why "The Shadow"?

A shadow is a shaded area made when light is blocked. There are many good reasons to make shadows the subject of your science project. For example:

Cost   Shadows are free. You don't need to buy, borrow, or photocopy one.

Everybody is a pro.   Unlike rock candy, balloon sculptures, and touchdowns, *anybody* can make a shadow.

Parents   No need to bug Dad or Mom for use of the power drill or oven. You can study shadows easily and safely. Just stand near a light or hang out on a sunny day.

Science is the study and explaining of stuff that happens in nature.

You live half your life in one.   Night is a shadow! When the Sun shines on one side of the Earth (day), the other side is in a shadow (night).

You can't forget it.   Ever work really hard on something and then forget to bring it to school? Don't you hate that?! No need to worry this time—your shadow goes wherever you do.

SHADOWS ARE FREE FOR YOU — AND ME!

THE BEST SHADOWS ALWAYS FOLLOW YOU!

Every shadow you see is just begging for scientific study.

Think about it . . .

- What are shadows?

- How do they keep us cool?

- Why are they sometimes so **big**, sometimes so small, sometimes just the **right size**, and sometimes not there at all?

- How can shadows be used to tell time?

- Can there be shadows at night?

- How do shadows enable us to see shape and texture?

See? The shadow is the perfect mixture of great fun and great science—a winning solution for most any science project.

Think Clearly: A Top Ten List

1 Before you do anything else, even before you go to the bathroom, **figure out what your project is**. Is it a group project? A written report? Two pages or five pages? Oral? Two minutes or five minutes?

2 **What do *you* have to do?** If you're working in a group, figure out what *you* have to do. (Even though it might not always seem like it, teachers know who the real slackers are in any group.)

3 Get started so you can get finished. Don't wait to start! You might get sick. You might get invited to a party. Stuff like this really happens.

Research: Allow five days, one hour every day.

Writing: For a **written** report , write two hours the first day. On the second day, rewrite (make it better!) for one hour. Take the next day off (you deserve it!). Rewrite for 30 minutes on the fourth day.

Practice: For an **oral** project , practice your presentation for three days. On the first day, practice it out loud behind closed doors once and once with a parent. On the second day, practice it once—with any changes from your parent—behind closed doors, once more for a parent, and one more time behind closed doors. On the third day, practice it one last time in private.

An **exhibit**  should be finished two days before it is due at school. Ask family members to check it out for you. Any problems with it? Tape coming off? Anything breaking? This leaves you one day to fix it.

4 Check the spelling on *everything*.

5 **Has somebody, like a family member, checked over everything?** Sometimes a different set of eyes sees stuff you don't.

6 **Is tomorrow the big day? Get a good night's rest.**

7 **Look one last time at your teacher's instructions.** Have you done *everything*?

8 Pack the night before. Is your exhibit big or fragile? Have you figured out a way to get it to school without wrecking it? Don't wait until the bus is outside honking its horn to figure out this packing stuff.

9 If you can, pee before class.

10 **Your contribution to this Top Ten List (whatever we forgot):**

_____

_____

Getting Started
(The Amazing Note Card)

For every project you must do one thing: collect information (also known as **research**). That's what a school project is all about: collecting information and presenting it to somebody. That somebody may be a teacher or other students.

So how do you collect all that information? With the amazing note card.

The Amazing Note Card

You can collect information about shadows, for example, by **reading** a book (like this one), a magazine, or a newspaper; **watching** a video or TV show; **searching** the Internet; or **interviewing** somebody (see page 61).

Whenever you find something interesting on your topic, write it down on a note card. Be sure to also write on the card where you found the information (for example: **My Life in the Shadows,** a book by Shady Moss, school library). Keep creating these cards until you have a stack of them.

Now arrange the cards in some order that makes sense. For example, cards on the same topic should be together. One card should follow another for good reason.

Imagine that if you taped all the cards together, like a string of cut-out dolls, you'd have a very rough first draft of a paper or presentation. **Neat, eh?**

On the next 13 pages are 44 note card-like pieces of information to get you started. Read through some of them. Go ahead, right now.

See how they don't read like a normal book or paper? That's because these note cards are just the beginning of your work. They are not yet in an order that makes any sense. They're still like a bunch of letters (W, S, O, A, D, H) that have to be put in order so that they make up a word (SHADOW).

For example, if you just copied these note cards out of the book and handed them to your teacher, the teacher would say something like, "That's a good start. NOW FINISH IT! Go write a paper that makes sense. These are just stones. Build a wall with them."

If this is a group project, think about how to share this note card work. Dividing it up by topic is a good way. Someone can research a *solar eclipse* (when the Moon casts a shadow on the Earth). Someone else may research the use of shadows to tell time. And someone else may find all the "extra" weird stuff on shadows. (Where's the world's longest shadow? Who is this old-time radio character known as "The Shadow"? etc.)

You can buy packs of note cards or cut paper into pieces about three inches high and five inches wide. (Use this paragraph's note card as a guide.) Keep your note cards in a paper clip, or, if you do a lot of research, a rubber band will work.

Really Helpful Hint:

Once you have a lot of note cards, you should figure out what information is really important, what is somewhat important, and what is not really important, but interesting. So review all your note cards and mark those that contain really important information. For example, over the next few pages we've marked those note cards that contain the really important information with an exclamation mark:

OK?

And, hey, good luck with your note cards!

1 ❗
Shine a flashlight on a wall. Now hold a pencil in the light. Look at the wall again. The pencil blocks light from reaching the wall, right? Light cannot go through the pencil. Anything that doesn't let light through—like you, this book, or your brother's head—is opaque. A shadow is wherever light does not shine because of something opaque.

2 ❗
What makes a shadow? Light + an opaque object + a surface. The shade of a tree is a shadow: the light is sunlight (+) the opaque object is the tree (+) the surface is the ground.

LIGHT

OPAQUE OBJECT

SHADOW

SURFACE

3
The opposite of opaque is transparent. Substances, like window glass, that allow light to travel through them are transparent.

13

How could a big fella like me have such a small shadow?

4 ❗
Changing the position of the light changes the shadow. When light shines down directly on an object, the shadow is short. Around noon, when the Sun is high in the sky, shadows are short and fat. Check it out. Shine a flashlight on something from above, then shine from the side. See how the shadow changes.

5
The Sun's like a really big flashlight. Early in the morning and late in the afternoon, when the Sun is low in the sky, shadows are long and thin.

6 ❗
Shine a flashlight on something (like a stuffed animal, coffee cup, or candlestick holder). Notice the shadow. Now shine a second flashlight on the object. See that? Change the number of lights and the number of shadows change. When two lights shine on you, you have two shadows.

7 ❗
Change your object. Replace it with something of a different shape. See how the shadow changes. Objects with different shapes have different shadows. Try something with a hole in the middle of it (like a bagel). In the shadow, can you make the hole disappear?

8 ❗

Change the surface on which the shadow is cast, and the shadow changes. Try a flat surface. Then steps (or stairs) and grass. A shadow zigs and zags as it bends around corners and up and down steps. Try a curved surface (like a big pot).

9

Imagine it's a sunny day and you're standing in the shadow of the Empire State Building. Do you cast a shadow? Nope. When a larger object blocks the light from shining on a smaller object, the smaller object has no shadow.

10

In a room lit only by a lamp, hold your hand close to the lamp (but not so close that your hand gets burned!). The shadow of your hand is huge, right? That's because your hand is shutting out a lot of the light. Move your hand away from the light. Then farther and farther away. The hand's shadow gets smaller and smaller and smaller, because your hand does not shut out so much of the light.

11

When you move, your shadow moves. When you run, your shadow runs. But you can never catch it.

HEY! WAIT UP!

12 ❗

On cloudy days, shadows are hard to find. This is because water particles in the air scatter the sunlight. Grab your flashlight and go to the bathroom. Turn the shower on and the lights off. Hold up a hand, shine the flashlight on it. Nice shadow, eh? Now shine the light at your hand through the shower water. Lousy shadow, right?

13 ❗

Shadows are useful. They help you know what shapes things have. Without the shadow on an egg, the egg would look flat—like a circle.

14 ❗

Shadows help you see the shape of things (like the Washington Monument).

Where is the sun for our shadows to look like this?

15a ❗
People have used shadows to tell time for thousands of years. On a sundial, as the Sun moves across the sky, a shadow "points" to the time of day on this simple clock's "dial."

15b

16 ❗
Sundials were used by people in ancient Greece, Rome, Egypt, and China. Unlike most modern clocks, a sundial has no moving parts. The part of the sundial that sticks up and casts the shadow is called a gnomon (NO-mun), which is Latin for "how one knows" (the time, that is!).

17 Make a shadow-stick "clock." Put clay in the center of a piece of cardboard (at least 10 x 10 inches) and stick a pencil in the clay. Place this outdoors in the Sun at 9 a.m. At the end of the pencil's shadow on the cardboard, write "9." Every hour, until the Sun sets, write the time (10, 11, etc.) at the end of the shadow. You can now use your "clock" on any sunny day. Remember, it gives the correct time only when it sits the same way, in the same place as when you first made it.

18 ❗
Do sundials and stick clocks work at night and on really cloudy days? No. Which is why we use the watches and clocks that we do.

19 In 10 B.C., Caesar Augustus, the first emperor of Rome, built a huge sundial. The hours of the day and the seasons of the year were inscribed on a plaza that was several thousand square feet. A 90-foot stone shaft (that's nine stories high!) served as a pointer. (The shaft was brought from Egypt, where it had been an offering to the Sun god.) On his birthday, at the precise hour of his birth, the pointer cast a shadow on an altar honoring Augustus.

20
Shadows are used to find directions without a compass. This is the easy way: On a sunny day drive a stick into the ground so that it makes no shadow. Within 15 or 20 minutes, a shadow will appear at the base of the stick. The shadow will always point to the east.

21a This is the difficult way: At around 11 a.m. on a sunny day, stick a pencil in the ground. Scratch a circle around the pencil using the length of the pencil's shadow as the radius. Mark with a pebble where the shadow and the circle meet. After an hour, check the pencil's shadow every few minutes. When the shadow has again grown long enough to touch the circle, mark that point with another pebble. Draw a straight line between the two pebbles. Now draw a line from the pencil to the line connecting the pebbles. This line points north.

21b

about 11 a.m.

N

22a

For more than a thousand years, people on the Indonesian islands of Java and Bali have enjoyed shadow puppet plays known as wayang. The puppets are made of pieces of stiff leather attached to thin sticks. Holes are cut in the leather to create facial features. The arms and legs are jointed so that they bend and move. A bright light behind the puppets projects their images onto a screen of thin white cloth.

22b

23 When a portrait photographer takes a photo of somebody, it's important to have just the right light. Not enough light, and the photo will be dark. Too much light, and the person's nose, cheekbones, or forehead may cast weird-looking shadows across the face. To have enough light but no shadows, photographers "backlight" their subjects: the photographer puts lights behind, and on each side of, the person being photographed. These lights keep the photo bright but block out any shadows.

Why does my shadow look so broken up?

24a
Hold two fingers in the light of a flashlight. Do you see the shadow of your fingers? Now hold up five fingers. Move them around. Make different shadow shapes with your fingers, like a bird's wings, a horse's head, and a quacking duck.

24b

25a ❗ The Moon has no light of its own. The Moon shines because it reflects light from the Sun. Sometimes the Earth gets directly between the Moon and the Sun. This causes Earth to block the Sun and cast a shadow on the Moon. This is called a lunar eclipse (<u>lunar</u> is Latin for "moon" and <u>eclipse</u> is Greek for "leave out"). During a lunar eclipse, the Earth's shadow makes the Moon look very dark for a while.

25b

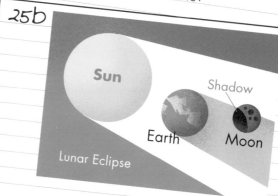

Sun

Shadow

Earth

Moon

Lunar Eclipse

26

During a lunar eclipse, the Earth's shadow on the Moon is <u>always</u> curved. Shine a lamp on a wall. Then try to find an object that <u>always</u> makes a round shadow, no matter how you hold it. How about a shoe? A box of cereal? This book? A ball? Only a ball <u>always</u> makes the round shadow.

27 ❗

Ancient Egyptian astronomers figured out the Earth was round long before explorers sailing around the world did. These astronomers realized that the only shape that makes a curved shadow—no matter how you shine light on it—is a ball.

28! A Greek astronomer, mathematician, and geographer, Eratosthenes (276 – 194 B.C.), looked at shadows and came to this conclusion: the Earth must be round. Eratosthenes saw that at noon in one city (Syene, now known as Aswan), <u>there were no shadows</u>; yet in another city further north (Alexandria), at the exact same time on the exact same day, <u>there were shadows</u>. This could happen only if the two cities were both sitting on something shaped like a ball.

29! Eratosthenes wasn't done. Using measure-ments of the shadows and some fancy math, he figured out that the distance between the two cities was one-fiftieth of the whole Earth. To then find the size of the entire Earth, he paid someone to walk from Alexandria to Syene count-ing his steps, then he multiplied that distance by 50. The answer he got was very close to the best modern measurements of the circumference of the Earth (about 25,000 miles). That was 2,200 years ago, and all that Eratosthenes used was a stick, shadows, and some arithmetic.

30! There are some big shadows visible on the Moon. Its craters are easiest to see along the line that divides the light side of the Moon from the darkened side. Here the mountains encircling the craters cast huge shadows that stand out against the nearby lighted areas.

31a ❗ In addition to lunar eclipses, there are solar eclipses. About once or twice a year, the Moon comes directly between the Sun and the Earth, and casts a shadow on the Earth. The long shadow of the Moon is like the pointed end of a pencil (see illustration). It may be only 50 to 100 miles across where it touches the Earth.

31b

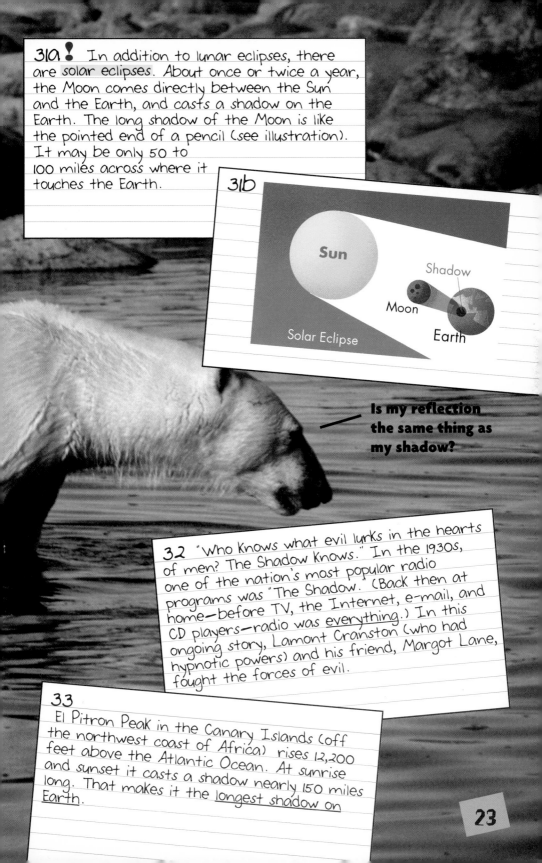

Sun

Shadow

Moon

Earth

Solar Eclipse

Is my reflection the same thing as my shadow?

32 "Who knows what evil lurks in the hearts of men? The Shadow knows." In the 1930s, one of the nation's most popular radio programs was "The Shadow." (Back then at home—before TV, the Internet, e-mail, and CD players—radio was <u>everything</u>.) In this ongoing story, Lamont Cranston (who had hypnotic powers) and his friend, Margot Lane, fought the forces of evil.

33
El Pitron Peak in the Canary Islands (off the northwest coast of Africa) rises 12,200 feet above the Atlantic Ocean. At sunrise and sunset it casts a shadow nearly 150 miles long. That makes it the <u>longest shadow</u> on Earth.

34
From an airplane,
you can see the large
shadows of windblown
clouds slowly move
across the land below.

35
When it's a cloudy day, you're living in
the shadow of all the clouds.

36
In places where it's completely cloudy,
people spend their day in a shadow that
may be hundreds of miles long.

37a Want to know how to draw distorted versions of favorite things? Go outside and find a place where you can see your shadow. Put a big piece of paper on a smooth sidewalk or table. Place the favorite thing—action figure, doll, cheeseburger, whatever—in the middle of the paper. Is the shadow normal? That's a bore. Wait an hour. Now how's the shadow? Tall, skinny, and goofy-looking? Great! Use a crayon to trace around the thing's shadow. Do you think your classmates would enjoy this?

37b

38a ❗ The Earth and the Moon are constantly traveling around the Sun. Sometimes the Moon passes between the Sun and the Earth, blocks the Sun's light, and casts a shadow on the Earth. If you're on part of the Earth in total shadow, the Sun is completely hidden by the Moon. This is a total eclipse of the Sun. Other parts of the Earth are in partial shadow, with a partial view of the Sun. In a total eclipse of the Sun, only the Sun's outer atmosphere shines around the Moon.

38b

HEY! LOOK WHO'S TRYIN' TO PASS ME!

39a

A silhouette is a shadow of your profile. (Your head seen from the side is your profile.) Sit so that a bright light casts a shadow of your profile onto paper. While you sit very still, have a friend trace the outline of your profile on the paper. Then cut out the tracing with scissors and fill it in with dark paper, ink, or crayon.

39b

Our shadows move and change shape as we move!

40

As long as you're not in a city with a lot of bright lights, you can have a shadow in a full Moon. If the Moon is bright and you're near another light, you may have two nighttime shadows.

41

The French artist August Edouart (1769 – 1861) did silhouettes of famous people such as Henry Wadsworth Longfellow, France's King Charles X, and American presidents Martin Van Buren and William H. Harrison. Edouart believed that shadow pictures of just the head could not represent a person's character, so his silhouettes were of the full body (head to toes!).

42a Shadows can help you create art. Place a piece of paper so that an object's shadow is cast on it. A sculpture or a small plant like a flower works well. For a plant, you may have to lay a heavy book next to it, then the paper on top of it. With a pencil, shade in or trace the shadow. Further shading with some watercolors will have you painting like a regular Michelangelo. Shadow art is easy, and you can do lots of it quickly. So it's a perfect way to spruce up a simple invitation, thank-you note, or school report.

42b

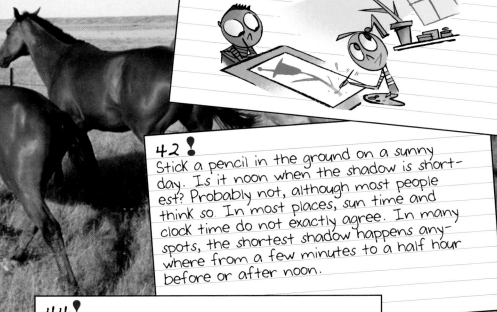

42 !
Stick a pencil in the ground on a sunny day. Is it noon when the shadow is shortest? Probably not, although most people think so. In most places, sun time and clock time do not exactly agree. In many spots, the shortest shadow happens anywhere from a few minutes to a half hour before or after noon.

44 !
The biggest shadow of all is night itself. It is then that you are in the shadow cast by the Earth. You spend a good part of your life in this shadow.

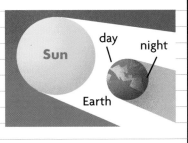

Sun day night Earth

Getting Your Dexters in a Row
(Setting Your Priorities)

Well, What about Shadows?

For your science project, are you going to present every-thing there is to know about shadows? Or are you going to focus on how to tell time and direction with shadows? Or how shadows lower temperature? Or how shadows prove that the Earth is round?

You've done some research by this point. What part of that information are you going to use? Or do you need to do more research?

Sample

Let's say you decide to focus your science project on using shadows to determine time and direction.

Go back to the note cards. Although the ones in this book are only a sampling, pretend they are all your note cards. Now mark those—go ahead, use a pencil, put a lit-tle check mark (✔) on each one—that you would use to prepare a short oral presentation. Remember, your shad-ows topic is "When and Where: Using Shadows to Tell Time and Direction."

To check your selection against ours, see page 64.

Organizing All the Information

Be very clear as to what your report is *about*. You do this by giving a title to your exhibit 🖼, or with the opening sentences of a paper 📄, or in the first few sentences of an oral report 📏.

This will be helpful to your listeners and readers. But, better yet, a clear understanding of what you're working on will be of great help to *you*. Once again, let's pretend your report topic is "When and Where: Using Shadows to Tell Time and Direction." You might want to write that down on a piece of paper and keep it in front of you.

Remember, in a paper or oral report, first clearly write what your topic is. Follow that with the information you collected and selected. And at the very end, sum up your topic in a couple of sentences.

Really Helpful Hints:

- This is a **science** project. Do not use goofy humor and hand shadow stuff as your main topic. At most, this fun stuff (also known as **trivia**) should be sprinkled in to pep up a report. A little goes a long way. Remember, your **science** teacher is looking for **scientific** information.

- Once you've picked the note cards from which you'll write your report, number them! Otherwise, dropping them might be a full-blown disaster.

- If you're doing an oral report and using note cards or sheets of paper, number them! That way, you won't worry about losing your place when you're in front of the class.

- If you will refer to a written paper during your oral report, make doing that as easy as possible. Print it out in large, easy-to-read letters

LIKE THIS.

3: TRIVIA DID YOU KNOW THAT CERTAIN PLANTS GROW BETTER IN THE SHADE?

Experiments and Activities

31

Discover the Shadow

Here's a series of small activities to be used for an oral report to your classmates. There's nothing here that will surprise them. You'll simply cause them to pause in the middle of a busy school day and think about shadows. Read through it, and then think about and write down what you might say as you do the activities. We did this for you in *italics* on the first two paragraphs. And then practice the activities to see if you can present them without notes. You really need to—both of your hands are going to be very busy. This should be fun!

You'll need two flashlights and a pencil. Here goes:

"Let's think about shadows." Darken the room. Not pitch black, just dark enough to cast shadows. *"What makes a shadow? Light plus an object plus a surface."*

Shine a flashlight on the wall. Place your open hand—as if you're waving—in the ray of light. *"The light goes around my hand. And the light goes between my fingers. But it can't go through my hand. The light shines on the wall except where my hand blocks out the light and makes a shadow."*

Put a pencil between your fingers so that it sticks out from your hand. Shine the flashlight so that it casts a shadow on your hand. Walk around the room so that all your classmates can see the shadow. As you do, hold the flashlight above the pencil (no shadow), then a bit to the pencil's side (short shadow), and then far to the pencil's side (long shadow). And keep talking. Show how a shadow changes depending on where the light is coming from.

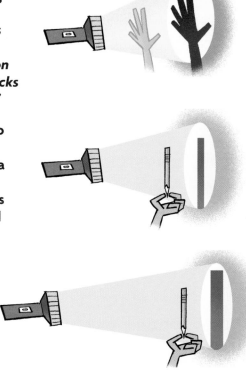

Lay one flashlight on a table and place your hand in the light to cast a shadow as you did earlier. Now, from lower than the table, shine the second flashlight at your hand. Two shadows of your hand will be cast on the wall. Show how changing the number of lights changes the number of shadows.

Move your hand so that it parallels the floor. Show how changing the position of an object changes the shadow. Note that every object has many different shadows. Place your open hand parallel to one wall, then the floor, then at an angle. Turn your hand into a fist.

Show how changing the surface on which a shadow is cast changes the shadow. Cast the shadow of your hand into the corner of the room where two walls meet.

Hold the flashlight at your chin and shine it up, at, and over your face to make it scary-looking. Then in an evil voice ask if there are any questions.

Clouds and Shadows

This is a simple experiment to determine how the shadows caused by clouds affect the Sun's strength. You might do this experiment several times, on different days, at different places, or at different times. Then include your findings in a written report.

What you need.

- two outdoor thermometers (check with your teacher—the school may have some thermometers for science classes)

- a sunny day (the sunnier, the better)

- a shadow (a large one, like the shade from a building or tree)

WARNING! Because some thermometers are made of glass and break easily, handle them carefully—very carefully! If you break a thermometer, don't touch it. Find an adult to do the cleanup (this is one of the reasons adults were invented).

What you do.

1 Read the thermometers first to be sure they have the same temperature.

2 Place one thermometer in the Sun.

3 Place the other in the shade.

4 Wait about ten minutes.

5 Check the temperature on both thermometers.

What's going on?!

The thermometer that was in the Sun ended up with the higher temperature. Why? Just as a shadow blocks the Sun's light, a shadow also blocks the Sun's heat. This is why it's cooler on a cloudy day than on a sunny day.

For a group project, imagine different locations to place the thermometers and compare their temperatures. For example, put one thermometer in the shadow of a leafy tree and the other in the shadow of a house. Put one in a morning shadow and the other in an evening shadow.

For an exhibit, place a lamp on a table. Put one thermometer directly in its light. Then create a shadow (use a box, for example) and place the other thermometer in the shadow. Post a note telling viewers to check the temperatures of each thermometer. Also post information on how shadows change temperature and be sure to refer to night and to cloudy days.

Helpful Hints:

1 Be sure there are electrical sockets for your exhibit (or check to see if you're going to need an extension cord); if not, you might be better off doing another exhibit. Have a teacher plug in any electrical cord for you.

2 If you can, tie or tape the thermometers to the table to keep them from falling to the floor and breaking.

3 Try all of this at home first!

Confused Shadows!

On the next two pages are drawings of confused shadows. They are drawn to do what shadows do **not** do. **The Handy Confusion Guide** on page 38 tells you what's out of whack with each drawing.

You can use Confused Shadows in several ways:

At the end of an oral report, you can hand out copies of the confused shadows (or better yet, draw your own!) and quiz your classmates to see what they've learned about shadows. You might break the class into teams of three or four and provide each team with a set of the confused shadows. After a few minutes, see which team knows their shadows best. (This is a great excuse to bring a prize, like cookies, to school.)

For a group project, each team member can draw three original confused shadows and use those. Or one of you could give a short report on shadows, another could prepare confused shadow drawings and hand them out, and another could run the contest.

For an exhibit, place copies of this book's confused shadows, or your own, on poster board. Challenge your exhibit visitor to figure out what is wrong with the shadow of each drawing. Place the answer sheet face down on the exhibit table, or hang it from the poster board. Be sure to write "ANSWERS" or "HANDY CONFUSION GUIDE" on the back of the answer sheet.

Confused Shadow A

Confused Shadow B

Confused Shadow C

Confused Shadow D

Confused Shadow E

Handy Confusion Guide

A The cat should have a shadow.

B Three trees of different heights need shadows of different lengths.

C The cow's shadow should point away from the Sun, not toward it.

D The flower shadows should be parallel and equal in length.

E The shadow cast by the light nearer to the six should be larger than the shadow cast by the more distant light.

The World's Biggest Shadow

It's not always easy to imagine that night is nothing more than the world's biggest shadow. But with this activity, you'll stick something like the Earth in front of something like the Sun and see what happens to some place like where you live.

What you need.

- a day sunny enough to cast shadows

- a globe of the Earth*

- if the globe is not on a stand, something to hold the globe (like an empty coffee can)

- clay (or Playdoh)

- two toothpicks (or really, really, really small toy people)

*Really Helpful Hint:

Don't have a globe? Check with your teacher—there's probably one in the school somewhere. Or ask friends, parents, and neighbors—some people even have inflatable beach balls that look like a globe. Or just use markers to draw the continents on an old soccer ball or basketball.

What you do.

1 Go outside during the day.

2 Set the globe in its holder. Turn the globe around until where you live is on top of the world.

3 Stick some clay (or Playdoh) on the spot where you live.

4 Stick a toothpick (or a really, really, really small toy person) in the clay. That's you!

5 THIS IS IMPORTANT: Look for your shadow on the ground next to you. Make sure the toothpick is casting a shadow in the same direction as your own shadow. Remember—keep moving the globe around until the toothpick's shadow is parallel to your own shadow.

6 Look at what you've created and start asking questions:

● Right now, where is it dark on the Earth? What people are now living in the shadow known as night?

● Where is the Sun now rising?

● Where is it now setting?

● Can you find a place on the Earth where it will be dark all day today?

- Can you find a place where the Sun will never set today?

- Where will the Sun be rising or setting an hour from now? Can't answer that? Wait half an hour and notice how the shadow has moved around the Earth. Now can you answer that question?

- Is it day or night or in Japan, Chicago, New York, Los Angeles, Hawaii, Alaska, Europe, Africa, and Orlando?

For an exhibit, you can set up your Earth and Sun models. You can title your exhibit "Night: The World's Biggest Shadow." Be sure to identify what time of the day it is and what is going on at that moment in other countries of the world.

Shadow Lab

This is a great activity for an oral report to your class. You're going to turn your classroom into a laboratory. And you're going to be the head scientist. If you can (check with your teacher), you might want to set up a table in the middle of the classroom and gather your classmates around it. Also check with parents and teachers to see if you can borrow a laboratory coat from somebody. Wearing one would be cool.

What you need.

- two flashlights (see Helpful Hint)
- a white sheet or tablecloth
- a room you can darken
- a small box, like a box of crayons
- a clear plastic measuring cup with painted lines
- a wine glass
- notebook paper
- scissors

Helpful Hint:

To make sharp, clear shadows, a small, bright light source—like a penlight or Mini-MagLite—works best. Most regular flashlights have reflectors that make a broad beam of light, which is nice if you want to find your way in the dark, but not as good if you want to make sharp-edged shadows.

What you do.

1 Put the sheet down on a table. Stand the box in the middle of the sheet. Turn on a penlight. Turn off all the other lights in the room.

2 Hold the penlight down on the table about a foot away from the box. Shine the light on the box, and slowly move the light up and over it (see illustration). Watch the shadow. Does the shadow stay the same shape as the box? Can you make the shadow bigger and smaller? Can you make the edges of the shadow sharp or fuzzy? What happens if you move the light in a circle around the box?

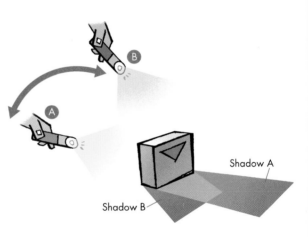

Shadow A

Shadow B

3 Shine the light on one side of the box. Now turn on the second flashlight, and shine it on the other side of the box (see illustration). How many shadows can you make? Can you make one shadow darker than the other?

4 Put the measuring cup on the table. Shine the light through it from the side (see illustration). Can you read the cup's markings in its shadow? Hold the light right over the cup, then move it down until it's inside the cup. What happens to the shadow?

5 Shine the light through the wine glass from the outside and inside. Now fill the glass with water and shine the light through it (see illustration). How does that change the shadow?

6 Make a snowflake from a square of paper (see illustration). Fold the square in half, then fold it in half again. Fold the little square into a triangle, then fold that triangle again, if you can. Cut little tiny snips out of the folded edges. Unfold it to make a snowflake. Place the snowflake over the wine glass and shine the light down through it. Move the light and watch how the shadows change.

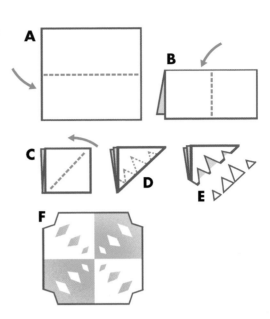

7 Loosely crumple up a piece of paper and put it down on the table. Move the light and watch how the shadows on the paper change.

8 Some other fun things to play with on your shadow table are combs, salt shakers, wax paper, facial tissue, glass bowls, and kitchen utensils such as forks, colanders, and spatulas.

Space Shadows

Remember that a lunar eclipse happens when the Earth gets between the Sun and the Moon, causing the Earth to cast a shadow on the Moon (see note cards 25a and b). If that's tough to imagine, this activity can help.

What you need.

- a large ball (like a beach ball or soccer ball)
- a small ball (like a Ping-Pong ball)
- a room you can darken
- tape or a rubber band
- a piece of string
- a flashlight or table lamp

What you do.

1 **Use the large ball for the Earth and the small ball as the Moon.**

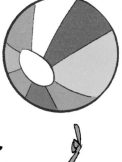

2 Use tape or a rubber band to stick a piece of string to the "Moon" so you can hang it in front of the "Earth. (See illustration.)

3 Use a flashlight or a table lamp as the Sun.

4 Can you make the Earth cast a shadow on the Moon? What happens to the shadow if you move the Moon in a circle around the Earth?

Interplanetary Shadows

If the Moon gets between the Sun and the Earth and causes an eclipse, why isn't there an eclipse whenever one of the other planets gets between the Earth and the Sun? In other words, does Mercury ever cast a shadow on us? Let's find out.

What you need.

- a desk lamp
- your thumb

What you do.

1 Stand about 2 yards from the desk lamp.

2 Close your right eye.

3 Hold your left thumb at arm's length in front of your left eye and in front of the lamp.

4 Slowly move your thumb toward your face until it is directly in front of your open eye.

Hey, what's going on?! Did you notice that the farther your thumb is from your eye, the smaller the thumb appears and the more of the lamp you see. The closer your thumb is to your face, the more light it blocks. Because Mercury is very close to the Sun, it blocks only a small portion of the Sun's light, just as your thumb did when held close to the lamp. The shadow made by Mercury is so small that it does not spread out enough to fall on the Earth, but disappears in space.

The Well-Formed Shadow

Ever notice how shadows are sometimes blurry (like those cast by large buildings on a hazy day) and sometimes perfectly formed (like when drawing a silhouette of your friend's head)? What's that all about? Here's an idea for checking it out.

What you need.

- a pencil
- a flashlight
- wax paper
- a rubber band

What you do.

1 In a darkened room, hold a pencil about a foot from the wall.

2 Hold a flashlight about a foot away from the pencil and shine it toward the pencil so that a shadow appears on the wall. Check out the shadow.

3 Now cover the front part of the flashlight with wax paper, using a rubber band to hold the wax paper in place. Check out the shadow.

4 Try other stuff! Move the pencil closer to and further from the wall—what happens to the shadow? Keep the pencil in the same place but move the flashlight closer and further away— what happens? What happens if you put several sheets of wax paper over the flash- light? What if you replace the wax paper with some fabric?

Hey, what's going on?! Without the wax paper, most of the light arrives at the wall. The wax paper, however, scatters the light and less of it arrives at the wall. This 1) decreases the light around the shadow, 2) makes the shadow fuzzy, and 3) causes the shadow to be not as dark.

Same thing with your shadow: it's fuzzier on an overcast day than on a clear day.

Shadow Shenanigans

At the beginning or end of an oral report, it's sometimes fun to have your classmates goof off a little bit. Here are some simple and fun Shadow Shenanigans. (By the way, *shenanigan* means "innocent mischief." See if you can use the word before the day's over.)

1 **Ever make a "light mask"?** Darken a room and shine a flashlight on your face. Hold the flashlight at your chin and aim it *up*. You probably look a bit mean or scary. What facial features stand out? See how the dark shadows create their own shapes on your face? Keep goofing. This time hold the flashlight to your forehead and aim it *down* at your face. Do you still look scary? Which parts of your face are now in light or in shadow? Try the sides of your face. Try two flashlights. Hey, you're halfway to being some fancy lighting director for a Hollywood film.

2 **Shadow math. Check out this drawing.**

Can you figure out the height of the flagpole by using the shadow lengths of the yardstick and flagpole?

Really Helpful Hints:

1 If you haven't learned enough math yet to do this, ask your teacher for help. Might you know how to do this by the end of the school year?

2 For an oral report, you might want to copy this drawing on the blackboard or make copies to hand out to your classmates.

Answer: The flagpole is thirty feet tall.

3 **Your private "planetarium."** Can you darken your classroom? If so, shine a flashlight through a colander and onto the ceiling. The shadows cast will make it look like your own private planetarium.

4 **Wacky shadow.** You need a fluorescent tube light (turn out all the other lights), a pencil, and a wall. Hold the pencil perpendicular to the light. There *is* a shadow, right? Now hold the pencil parallel to the light. There's *no* shadow, right? That's wacky. What's going on? The shadow disappears because light from the ends of the tube falls on the places where the shadow should be and cancels out the shadow.

5 **Some kid being weird.** Some kid on the California coast is having lunch and watching the San Francisco 49ers play the Miami Dolphins on TV. The Dolphins' field-goal team comes out onto the field. Suddenly, the kid jumps up, heads outside, runs over to the high school football field, looks at it, pauses, then quickly returns home. What was that all about? *Answer on page 63.*

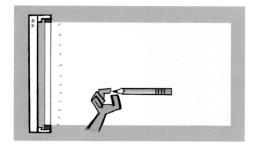

Really Helpful Hint:

For an oral report, you might want to write the above on a blackboard or hand out copies of it to your classmates.

Really Helpful Stuff!

These next five pages are here for you to use as you wish. That's right!—just go ahead and trace or photocopy these pages. You can then glue or tape them into a written presentation, copy and distribute them to your classmates, or attach them to a poster. It's up to you.

Robert Louis Stevenson (1850–1894) wrote adventurous, often scary books like *Treasure Island, Kidnapped,* and *The Strange Case of Dr. Jekyll and Mr. Hyde.* But he also wrote "My Shadow," a pretty neat poem about anybody's shadow.

MY SHADOW
by Robert Louis Stevenson

I have a little shadow that goes in and out with me,
And what can be the use of him is more than I can see.
He is very, very like me from the heels up to the head;
And I see him jump before me, when I jump into my bed.

The funniest thing about him is the way he likes to grow—
Not at all like proper children, which is always very slow;
For he sometimes shoots up taller like an India-rubber ball,
And he sometimes gets so little that there's none of him at all.

He hasn't got a notion of how children ought to play,
And can only make a fool of me in every sort of way.
He stays so close beside me, he's a coward you can see;
I'd think shame to stick to nursie as that shadow sticks to me!

One morning, very early, before the sun was up,
I rose and found the shining dew on every buttercup;
But my lazy little shadow, like an arrant sleepy-head,
Had stayed at home behind me and was fast asleep in bed.

Shadow ID

Look carefully at these shadows. Can you guess what object is making the shadow?

A

B

C

D

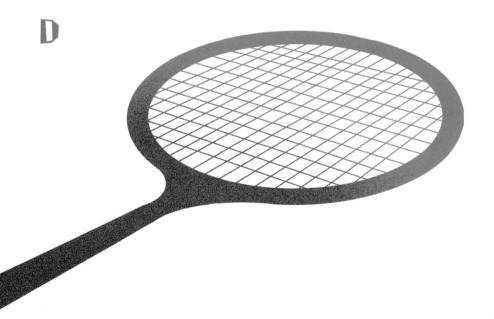

57

E

F

Answers: **A.** bowling pin and ball, **B.** CD, **C.** mailbox,
D. tennis racket, **E.** sail, **F.** Statue of Liberty

An Eclipse—
One Really BIG Shadow!

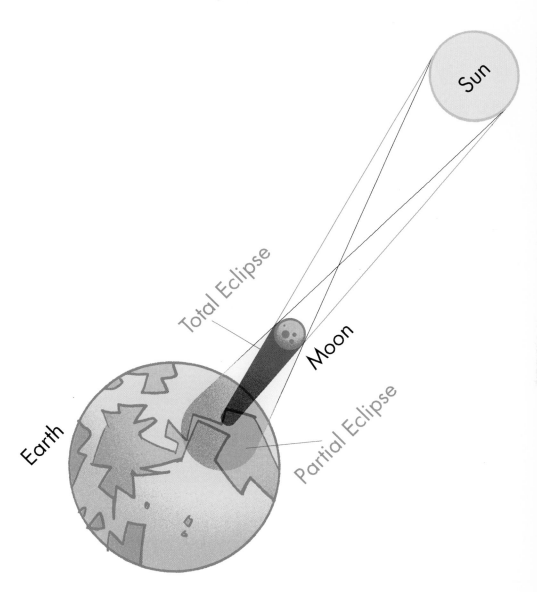

Sun

Total Eclipse

Moon

Partial Eclipse

Earth

The Sundial—
A Very Timely Shadow!

1 Cut out the face.

2 Cut an opening along the dotted line.

3 Cut out the arm.

4 Fold arm, bringing two halves together.

5 Insert arm through opening.

6 Tape A and B through back of sundial, like this—

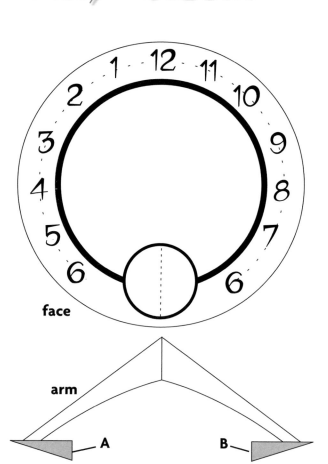

face

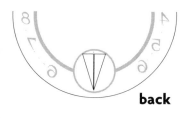

back

arm

A

B

7 Apply tape where necessary.

8 It should look like this—

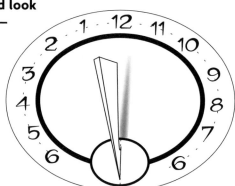

"Shadowy" People to Interview

You often will learn more and have more fun inter-viewing people than you will doing any other type of research. When you actually interview people instead of reading books and magazines about those peo-ple, they are called *primary sources.* In discovering the sci-ence of shadows, think about interviewing people who may work with, or have special knowledge of, shadows. Like the following people:

Really Helpful Hint:
Teachers love it when you use primary sources.

electrician

lighting-store staff

architect

landscaper

art teacher

illustrator

ophthalmologist

optometrist

photographer

makeup artist

interior decorator

window dresser

Additional Sources

Following are some of the books we discovered while learning about the science of shadows. Most are available at your school or public library. You and a helpful librarian are likely to find other books that we missed. When searching the library, keep key words like the following in mind: "shadows," "eclipse," and "sundial."

Bulla, Clyde Robert. **What Makes a Shadow?** New York: Thomas Y. Crowell, 1962.

Freeman, Ira M. **All About Light and Radiation**. New York: Random House, 1965.

Gardner, Robert, and Webster, David. **Shadow Science**. Garden City, New York: Doubleday, 1976.

Goor, Ron and Nancy. **Shadows: Here, There, and Everywhere**. New York: Thomas Y. Crowell, 1981.

Gregoire, Tanya, with Wilcox, Joan Parisi. **Museum of Science Activities for Kids**. Holbrook, Massachusetts: Adams Media Corporation, 1996.

Murphy, Pat, et al. **The Science Explorer Out and About**. New York: Henry Holt and Company, 1997.

Nye, Bill. **Bill Nye the Science Guy's Big Blast of Science.** Reading, Massachusetts: Addison-Wesley, 1993.

Popelka, Susan. **Super Science with Simple Stuff!** Palo Alto, California: Dale Seymour Publications, 1997.

Potter, Jean. **Science in Seconds at the Beach**. New York: John Wiley & Sons, 1998.

Taylor, Barbara. **Seeing Is Not Believing!** New York: Random House, 1991.

Van Cleave, Janice. **201 Awesome, Magical, Bizarre, and Incredible Experiments.** New York: John Wiley & Sons, 1994.

Whyman, Kathryn. **Rainbows to Lasers**. London: Gloucester Press, 1990.

And while at the library . . .

Search beyond books. Check out the magazines, newspapers, videos, and microfilm catalogs.

Internet

Search key words such as:

eclipse

shade

shadows

sundial

Answer from page 54: He was checking out the goal post's shadow to see if the game was being played in San Francisco or Miami. So does he know? Yes, in Miami. How'd he figure that out? He knows shadows. On TV, the goal post cast a shadow of over 20 feet. Yet the one at his local field cast one of only 5 feet. That means the Dolphins are kicking at a goal post that's way, way out in the Pacific somewhere where the Earth is just turning into the Sun (sunrise) or on the East Coast where the Earth is turning toward the Sun (sunset). Since the 49ers and Dolphins don't play in Fuji or Hawaii, the kid knows it's gotta be an afternoon game on the East Coast.

Hairy Science

Hair-ily perfect for school science projects! Discover, experiment, and report on genetics (Will I go bald?), zoology (What do hair, feathers, and fur have in common?), evolution (Why do you take your head in for a haircut and not your foot or elbow?), and anatomy (What's hair made of?).

Bouncing Science

Why does a Super Ball bounce so high? Why can you throw a baseball farther than a Ping-Pong ball but you can't throw a shot put farther than a baseball? How do tennis players make balls spin? And why can't you bowl on the beach? These and many other questions are researched and discovered in this well-rounded science project book.

Thumbs Up Science

While guiding the reader through scientific research into the human opposable thumb, Thumbs Up Science provides lots of activities, including "Thumb Essentials" (secrets behind tendon-driven hand movements) and "Thumb Fun" (palmistry and thumb wrestling).

Suggestion Selection (see "Getting Your Dexters in a Row," page 28):

If we were preparing a report on "When and Where: Using Shadows to Tell Time and Direction," we would pull the following note cards out of those provided: 4, 5, 15a, 15b, 16, 17, 18, 19, 20a, 20b, 21a, 21b, and 43.